Words
Unspoken

Tronell Walker

ISBN-13: 978-1080010394

Editing / Interior Book Design & Layout / Publishing Assistance:
CBM Christian Book Editing
www.christian-book-editing.com

Printed in the United States of America

Dedication

I dedicate my book to my angels, my sons, Tavon Gabriel Walker, Jr. and Trevez Gabrion Walker. You are both my inspiration and my reason for striving for excellence. The life I hope for your future led me to search for my purpose in life. My hope is that this book reveals to you both and all that read this book, that nothing in life is impossible.

By sharing my journey with the world, it is also my hope to provide information to choose rightly by having the Word of God and His influence in your life, so that there may be protection from many paths that I took myself.

May this book also bring inspiration to others who have walked similar paths.

To all my family and friends who supported me and believed in my dream being a reality, I truly thank you all.

To my grandmother who opened my eyes after you left this world, I set out to make you proud of me. Knowing you look down upon me every day of my life.

Most of all I am thankful to God for guiding my steps and loving me through it all. He has blessed my family and I, continuously giving us all a reason to keep going.

I gave *Unspoken Words* my whole heart in hopes of being a source of inspiration.

Be blessed and realize it is never too late!

TABLE OF CONTENTS

Introduction

Everyone has a story, and no two walks of life are the same. Therefore, I ask, *is one greater than the next?* I give you my story of overcoming, judgement, addictions, and mistakes made in the past from the things in life that were too hard to speak of, also including how I overcame each obstacle, hinderance or defeat. Life certainly can be difficult but also rewarding if you stick to what you believe in.

Remaining true to yourself can create a different story, igniting a fire inside to turn it all around. Staying true to who you are regardless of the flaws you see when you look in the mirror, or opinions others may have of you can be powerful in your life. Additionally, learning and knowing your identity in Christ will enable you to be capable of understanding that you are a beloved child of God.

Through it all, I have learned from many experiences in my life that God will keep you, no matter where you have been. Depending on the path chosen for you and the hardships you have to endure in life, it can make or break your faith. There are tests and trials; and it is important to know the difference. God is always the only one who feels your pain and knows your heart when no one else does through all the broken bridges. Some you may have broken on your own and the others you may have had no control over.

My intention is to inspire and give my life as an offering to unleash the dreamer in you. Thus, leading the way to a better and more powerful you. Loving yourself for not being perfect can shine a light no one can dim. It even brings closure to relationships God intended to end and also rebuilds the ones meant to last a lifetime. Everything will always work out in the end. Nothing in life is unattainable if you believe in your heart you are meant to be great. Having faith in knowing you have a purpose in life, great you will become. Having a constant mindset of a winner is the mindset needed. Victory is for everyone. What matters the most is how you perceive life, your own attitude, and how you handle it. Your life's purpose was already written, and God equipped inside of you everything you need to withstand your lessons and trials until you reach the promise, your purpose.

God put this book in my heart, and I give it to you, the reader. I hope and pray that this book can be an example of dreams that can and will come true, if you pursue them with God on your side. Life is living with a purpose.

Chapter One

The Beginning

Coming from a large family I, Tronell D. Thomas, am the oldest of six children from Destrehan, Louisiana. We are a family of four girls and two boys. We also come from a two-parent home. Being the oldest of the siblings, I grew up fast, wanting to help my mother take care of my siblings. Having that many personalities under one roof gave way for not one day of not having something going on. Whether it be arguments, parties, nagging each other, or blowing up the upstairs bathroom toilet. We are all close, surprisingly, but did have our share of disagreements. Family has always been and still remains one of my greatest passions. Even frustration from time-to-time, which is completely normal for a family my size. People have small families and find it extremely hard to stay close, so imagine having to share everything growing up with that many siblings. One case in point is that we all still can be friends and siblings always, having the best of both worlds.

As a little girl it was instilled in me that little girls are to be pretty, keep themselves up and have nice things. Be a lady, developing my mini-addiction to shopping. As well as loving to have nice jewelry all the time and shoes. I will pass up many gifts, even the most lavish ones, for the right pair of shoes. Begging my mom to wear her big earrings, which were the big thing back in the 80s. I was also a daddy's girl, so spoiled by him all the time. There were also countless trips to the store due to having a habit of standing on the sides of my shoes. Thankfully, for me, it took a while to break out of it.

Looking back, it amazes me how they managed to support a life for six children that involved trips every weekend, gifts and any activity we wanted to try as far as recreation, which was not limited to school activities as well. Almost every weekend we went somewhere like Chuck-e-Cheese, or took a drive to the Baton Rouge outlet mall for shopping.

My passion for life and beautiful things always kept a longing inside of me to be somewhere else. My first experience being on stage happened when I was at Norco Elementary School, a Christmas play. The excitement from being the center of attention in the play, even though the part wasn't the largest one, gave the hunger to want to be noticed. Moments like those paved the way for me wanting to be a star, or at least be seen. In my childhood, I wanted my voice to be heard by everyone, and in my family I was always the loud one.

My responsibility of being an older sibling also gave me the drive to learn how to cook, clean, and take on being the one in charge. I loved being in charge! I was always jumping at the chance to do something important, not limited to hanging Christmas lights from the roof of a two-story apartment building. Each responsibility installed a drive in me to be better at everything I was taught, and this was what I loved doing. Throughout my childhood life skating, drawing, music, and singing were passions of mine as well. I am proud to say they still are.

I made sure in school to take classes to prepare me for the life I wanted to live, or at least knew I was meant to live. I took Home Economics, Cooking, TV Production, and Art. I made sure that I was always one of the students to have a part in the plays read in English classes. The only classes I didn't mind being invisible in, was any type of math class. I could almost guarantee you that I would be finding ways to go help someone outside the room or doodling. If you put money in front of me, or need numbers crunched for some type of business, I can do it but never just for the love of math. I also took Chorus in my elementary days, elevating all the way to Honor Chorus, singing at events such as Christmas in the Oaks and every event that called for the chorus in school itself. Singing was an obsession for me. Whether it be school, home, shower, grocery store or anywhere for that matter, I made it my priority to learn every detail of it from stage presence to clef notes, pitches, and, though I have a disorder called "no rhythm from every now and then," I still learned dance moves. I guess I was not blessed with that ability.

I loved singing so much that one of my best friends throughout all my adolescent life, and still is to this day, started a singing group together. The group lasted all but one song but still one of my memorable moments. My lifelong philosophy is I will try almost anything at least once. Writing a lot of the music myself, and the rest my best friend, we sat together brainstorming or came together throwing our own ideas at each other that we had come up with on our own were special memories. We both had that star mentality shining through again and again. Having people singing along to the songs that I poured my heart into, using my music to do the exact same thing as I did growing up, helped me work through life as well.

I still remember the song we sang in the recording studio, "Boy You've Got Me." Unfortunately, that journey ended horrific for me. The journal I wrote my music in and had my life story in was given away. As I was told, as a down payment for the recording session. This was a tremendous price to pay because my source for writing is to mark those moments in my life that affected me in some type of way, or to let out the emotions I didn't allow to come through. This was my diary, so to speak.

Greed caused the people to keep it while seeing my name all throughout the journal. When I write I put the date and sometimes the time I wrote it, but definitely my name was on everything. With them keeping it, and I do know who has it, family, it can never be proved I wrote any of it. Why? The outcome was a record from my music and my heart. The world heard my music on a technicality. There is no way they will ever do what's right and admit that as long as there is no other way to prove it for as long as they have my work. God knows and as I work through life, I remind myself that God knows the truth, so one will be blessed when it's your winning season.

I am also fueled by the love for anything I do, and although money is important in life, it is my belief that you have to love what you do. I was not focused enough for it at the time, knowing what I know now though I was meant for something else. You never know your purpose in life if you don't apply yourself and continue to take those risks, breaking away from the normal everyday activities.

I was one of the only black girl's rollerblading around the neighborhood; that was just how different I was from everyone. I escaped many days to be alone to write and watch water behind the levees. In deep thought and as much as I enjoyed being around people, I enjoyed being

12

alone as well. Silence always fueled my creativity. Stopping at the corner store to buy snacks, or taking them from our cabinets at home, I would head off with my CD player, notebooks, and pencils. Doodling, writing poetry, and listening to the old school music, I was a young woman with an old soul and was not short of attention. Writing became a way to express the feelings I had trouble communicating with my actual words. Having five other siblings I did not have privacy as often as I would have liked. Finding places to be alone, I was an expert at it. Given the right situation in my adult life, I'm pretty sure I could disappear for a while with ease. Being a mother, I would have to pray I still have children when I returned from my quiet place! (I am laughing on the inside and outside.)

Watching the water and listening to all the sounds, falling in love with nature, getting caught up, losing track of time...this is where my love for butterflies came from. They stand for hope and love. I thought everything I am is in the meaning of this one creature. Gentle, vibrant, and some can be deadly. It is an actual fact there is a poisonous butterfly. It's important to pay attention to the details and make the connections from the information I am giving you about myself. Notice each phase, hear the passion, and notice the change. Trust me I am getting somewhere, not just rambling on and on about myself.

Then I was military bound; I was smart, sassy, and always the helpful one. My heart was always bigger than my body at times. I have compassion for everyone, and it compels me to give whenever I can. Sometimes when I can't pull change to amount to a dollar to give to the children collecting money for recreational trips (a habit of putting others before myself, a habit you truly need to be careful with). Putting the wrong people before yourself can lead to your destruction. I was obedient as well, at least that's what they all thought. That obedience I exhibited to others unwillingly at times going against what I wanted or loved, created a beast inside me that grew dangerously throughout the years. Every time my heart was broken, and failure, or disappoint came, I would be willing to do any and everything for the ones I loved came a dark side of me that began to grow. Behind every light, darkness does follows. God has to give you a story in order to have one to tell. That dark side took me to many places, and He has protected when I went every time.

Throughout my childhood life I attended church frequently with my grandmother. A church meant for Jehovah's witnesses, a religion that does not have the same beliefs as a normal Baptist church. They do not celebrate holidays, birthdays and many other things. I attended with one of my uncles, who I loved being around for his artistic vision as well. He was able to build ships with just matchsticks and glue. I went to church with his girlfriend many times. When I became older and stopped agreeing with the views of my grandmother's church, I still attended whenever I could. Unfortunately, when you deal with unspoken demons, nothing in life is consistent, there is always long periods of nothing but clamor. I have been to different churches looking for something, a place I can give God glory without feeling people whispering about you. I do know you should not let fear keep you from church, but you also need to agree with the way you feel sometimes.

My junior high school days is when my attitude and my light started to fade. This caused me to begin to lose sight of my dreams. My heart and giving spirit sometimes felt as a gift and a curse. I always was expecting people to feel the same way that I did.

With regard to the let downs one faces in life, I had trouble moving on from past hurts and traumas in my own life. With that said, I had more trouble in doing so and letting go. I held onto a lot of pain. Although, I still held on to faith, even though it slipped at those times when I questioned to myself, *why me?* From those moments, we as a "people" in which I am referring to the inner-self and thought life of a person, tend to live quietly for various reasons. Your mental health is however equally as important to align along with your attitude. It is this inner attitude that determines your place and purpose in life.

I was continuously active in high school, joining JROTC (Junior Officers Training Corps) for three years straight. I marched in bands, attended snake school (sleeping in the woods for three days) and went on field trips to different places. My admiration for the military stemmed from an uncle being in the military. (Not to mention the handsome drill sergeants yelling commands at me.) Being in the military was not like the instructors at school; it only took one time to pull up into the woods scared out of my mind, thinking, *what the hell is going on,* while listening to the Sergeant's scream at us to get off the bus, and looking around to see if this was a terrible idea. Once the dust settled and we were off the bus, I was in love and repelling off of a 500-foot-wall, or greater. Loving it and all that pain I felt later. I admired the way I looked from all the physical activity as well. I also recall taking trips to the bases that my uncle was stationed at as a teenager, and I also moved in with a cousin, who for a short period of time, as I helped him go a-wall being the getaway driver. Let me get back to the review of my life, and back to the basics of how my life began on a crash course into destruction.

I never completed high school because of those days, as the demons won. I would be skipping school, getting high, and drinking. When I was actually in school, we had late days, and on a few of them I was in the car with my friends, riding to see some guys we met, getting high instead of preparing for school. Even though I went right to get my GED, graduating before my class did, I wish I would have had the courage to talk to someone about how I was feeling. Considering that is not even the half of my story. I wish I had even tried a little harder to accomplish what I worked so hard for all my young life in school.

With that said, life happens and sometimes takes you to a place where you feel all hope is gone and misunderstood from not handling your issues correctly or being handled wrong. When you are a teenage it's easy to let all those feelings consume you mentally with the physical not being far behind.

In order to accept your purpose and be able to appreciate the blessings God has for you, I believe there is a season of crushing. My crushing season was 2017. I thought everything I had been through in my life before was the only thing holding me captive from achieving greatness; I was wrong. I repeatedly said 2017 was the worst year of my life. Relationships were destroyed, money was going, there was no transportation, I had also lost my husband. From that, I fell into an endless wave of depression, time after time, I would climb my way out, only to fall back in the pit of despair. I constantly prayed to God for answers, for angels to be released in my favor to help me out of it. Now, I recognize that year for what it truly was, my crushing season. I was being prepared and taught valuable lessons allowing me to be the woman I am, and destined to be.

I am now comfortable talking about the places I have been and the situations I have overcame. The clarity it has given me is unbelievable, opening not only my mind, but that season prepared my heart to accept all the blessings I am now ready for. I pray for anyone that has been through even one of my trials, to know every path does have a purpose.

Chapter Two

Stolen Innocence

I will say life is always unexpected, and looking back I have forced myself to remember the memories and bring them to the surface, so to speak out to others to help them does take courage, and for one to be fearless of what others might say or think. With an open heart, I share my testimony to help readers understand what can happen to young girls when their innocence is stolen or given away at the wrong time.

At an early age in life, I lost my virginity to an older family member. I suppressed it, and truly believed I lost my virginity later on in my teenage years. In actuality it was at a young age and somewhere in the back of my kind being, a child, and him being a family member, I felt it was right, normal even. In no way do I blame my parents for it, children will get into trouble fast without the parents being aware of it. Not talking about it, and going on with life, is how I handled many of my past childhood traumas that I went through. I don't want to put out an image that I am looking for sympathy by exposing everything that I went through as a young child/teenager. I overcame it all and worked through it. I am simply showing that nothing is too great to recover from. Take my struggles to help you conquer your own.

A darkness found me in my junior high school days in the form of a familiar face, that changed me for a long time. Not a stranger, the trauma would have been lesser if it happened to be one. From the first time meeting him, his energy never was right to me. He became part of the family through being the partner of one of the members of my family.

When I was young, I always loved to dress nice. One of the neighborhood friends, also considered family, complimented a friend and I on the way we carried ourselves, often. She would always say that we didn't dress too provocatively. We had the perfect balance: showing skin but still covered up. I felt at home in my surroundings; meaning a place where I felt love and knew everyone. Can you imagine a place where you never feel like you have to hide or worry about anything happening to you? That's what my comfort zone was for me. This was me in my neighborhood. When I was growing up, if a child went outside, the whole block was keeping an eye on that child. If you messed up, mom knew about it before she made it home. We would clock exactly what time to anticipate her car turning the corner, but even before she would arrive home, we were safe. During the time of my childhood, everyone was more open toward one another. We had an unspoken knowledge of who we were. We were family without being genetically related.

I was an attention grabber everywhere I went. The older men would wish they were younger to have a chance with me, and they actually told me that. The men were watching me, and they would start small talk, simply trying to see if I would give them a chance to be with me. Why they thought that? Only God knows.

I was outgoing, but I was still reserved. I loved being with family and with friends, but my thoughts were my own. I could discern who people really were early upon meeting them. So, early on I saw his twisted lust for me. I did not like the way he stared at me or talked about certain things around me. Later on, down the line, I discovered he had an addiction. He battled with substance abuse.

In the end, my hate for him proved right because I was violated; he tried to rape me. At first, I was in disbelief from it actually being real. What would cause a man to consider a child an object of affection? The dramatic event of this can hold you captive in your own mind. You try to convince yourself that it's not your fault it happened and working through it is your only option. I felt as if the winds were ripped from beneath my sails. He was robbing me of my innocence. As an adult, I came to the realization it actually was gone before it happened. Having been touched inappropriately by a cousin. Doing what only adults should have done.

It's something how news can travel really fast. Word of this incident got out. I was hearing remarks like, "You're a liar," and "You wanted it to happen." This is what he did, and after it happened, I felt he wanted to finish the job. I was feeling as if he was following me around. I was seeing him in places I know he really didn't have to be.

I started to smoke marijuana, drink alcohol, and take pills. I really turned my back on my sexuality being sacred. Promiscuity was an understatement for what became of me afterwards. I looked for affection wherever I could, and I didn't trust men afterwards. If all they wanted was sex, I gave it to them, but not just anyone. Certain men, men with money to be accurate. I don't know why I did this, because I always made my own money. At the age of fifteen going on sixteen, I had my own job. I made sure I always had my own money and could provide for myself. Some of the men I talked to was because they were nice. I cared less and less as the years went by about many things in my life. I also never spoke to anyone about how I felt, although I did mention I felt I was being watched what seemed as almost everywhere I went but since it looked as if it wouldn't change anything, I got high instead, focusing my attention on having fun. I was afraid, and uncomfortable in many of the places I went.

My coping mechanisms made dealing with it, a whole lot better, not feeling the pain was a way to forget about the emotions you suppress. I moved away from home numerous times, rebelling often and spent a lot of time away from family. Relationships changed and my life changed and that aided in me leaving home. I at first became roommates with a friend I met on my first job. Then later on down the line, allowing a friend to be my roommate became too much to handle and the daddy's girl relationship I once had was gone. I was constantly bumping heads with my father. Being an adult and having children, I realize now that I have a hard time looking back at all the mistakes I made and I also cry about what I went through, but just imagine how he (my father) felt watching his first daughter throw her life away.

Along my spiral downward, I have had two of the men I slept with, one a one night stand, and the other I had feelings for, that formed into short lived relationships. One was shot dead before he could make it to college on a baseball scholarship and the other that I cared for over-dosed, losing his life too soon. Leaving me to feel like maybe I was bad luck. When you feel you have already been through traumatizing events and that follows it, it adds to the trauma. Holding on to everything, a pile up growing with nowhere to go. Through all of the one night stands and wild adventures I will repeat because I know, God was there. After a night of drinking a suitcase of beer on my own and jumping into my friends Camaro to pick her up I fell asleep behind the wheel for close to a mile. The moments where you know you were supposed to be dead for sure or in worse condition other than waking up without a scratch. Nothing but God can be the explanation.

Went from innocent teen summit events, skating rinks, and movie trips doing what a normal preteen do to getting into cars with men going to their place. I am not in any shape or form racist, so I encountered men from different nationalities. I kept myself up going to nail shops every other week, hair styles changing every week or when my mood changed. Eating at places females my age where waiting to be able to go when they became of age. Distancing myself from my community and living a large part of my life out in New Orleans. Where many average people were afraid to go due to the whole city of sin complex.

My life had purpose, my life had promise but I let everything I went through take it away. No longer passionate about art, music, writing or being the star, I always knew I could be. I felt like I was just another person headed nowhere fast. Somewhere in the mist of it all I tried to end my life and thankfully without success. The idea of where I was headed scared me more than the problems I was facing, for taking your own life we all know it is hell. Partying, getting high, and living life as if I didn't value others' lives. or even mine.

There is always hope even when your life seems to have no purpose. Sometimes the worst days of your life can lead you to the best days of it as well. A story waiting to be told and as Maya Angelou said, "There is no greater agony than an untold story inside you." All the trauma I had experienced led to the path that I'm on now, and I thankful for them all.

Chapter Three

Building Blocks

As you get older the relationships you once had growing up with family members and friends will appear to fade away. These relationships may grow apart, as your own individual life develops. While maturing into the men and women you're destined to become, there are lies, secret struggles, miscommunication, and losing the glue that holds everyone together later on through the circle of life. Even through the long days that are without hearing or seeing each other as well. The same people you've known your whole life are barely spoken to and you know nothing about them as adults. I was always close to family, but I am guilty of letting life get in the way of many of my relationships. I still love them for who they are, my family. When you come from a place, when you were younger of course, knowing everything about each other, it seems as one gets older, there are things learned along the way that are not meant to be said. It's not ideal for everyone to know every aspect or detail about your life.

Everyone has expectations of you and it's hard to live up to those expectations. Family is what everyone holds dear to them and all family relationships start off as a unit loving and unbreakable. They are always there for each other in times of need and feeling like nothing can break that bond. When family comes to mind, I remember those cookouts where everyone is there laughing and joking, coming together as one. Arguments where far in between due to the love shared between each other. The way the world operates now is completely different, anything can cause a problem between any relationship.

The glue of all family's homes was always the gathering spot on major holidays, and for many still to this day, Grandma. A woman that sparks something inside of you with love unexplainable, still getting you in line when she needs to. Through her life, my own grandmother still works in my life through spirit. Laughing at crazy uncles who couldn't control themselves and whom loved being the life of the party. I remember running around the yard with cousins and looking forward to those living room sleepovers on top of each other. It was no secret that grandma was always the first on the babysitting call list.

As life goes on, as it should, the glue that held everyone together prepares to start another journey through the circle of life. I lost my grandmother a few years ago, January 20, 2011. Having lost my grandmother is one of the main reasons for the changes I am making in my life and have made, (emphasis on being one of the reasons). When the hurt went away, I said, *Oh my God, she can see what I'm doing.* I knew it was time to find my passion and make my mark in this world. I focused on the fact she is in a better place and is watching me. That knowledge created a wave and I have been working to be better day-by-day ever since. My only regret is not walking in my purpose before she left this world physically, but I know she is smiling down on me.

Family relationships crumble through individual struggle and the pain of losing the tie that binds. When there is already distance between family, losing someone of that magnitude adds fuel to the fire. There is no time to focus on working anything out when you are dealing with losing someone. Even though it can bring many closer together as well. Everyone has to deal with the loss in their own way. Also, the things you don't say to each other are creating more distance. Family is everything and going through your season without family is hard. I have been there going through the worst of times and feeling alone.

Relationships with siblings are probably one of the hardest to maintain during your periods of growth. In my case, I can reiterate that I was not walking in my purpose, but I was walking the path that was meant for me. All the turmoil pathed the way to my purpose; along the road I felt as though I failed as the older sibling. I also watched everyone pass me up in life, which is a mistake measuring my life to anyone else's.

It's easy to believe everyone stays the same and you get accustomed to the person you remember growing up. Through it all it is important to know everyone is dealing with their own battles in life. Understanding each person has their own walk in life and no two are the same.

Drugs, abuse, heartbreak, incarceration and losing loved ones, these are constant plagues that will forever be a present struggle factor for many people throughout life, that can alter the fabric of who you are. For every problem, each of us have our own ways of coping with them. Having that embedded in your mind, can change the way you interact with people on a daily basis. A smile can make a difference, saying hello, or simply asking how their day went.

Family has become an option to the world when family is what it needs the most, unity. Having someone there to catch you when you fall at times you didn't even know you were. Opening up like I'm doing, now can solve problems that can seem impossible to figure out. Well maybe not on such a large scale but anything is possible.

Holding on to past grudges only hurts yourself and closes the door for our children. If the adults are feuding, our children are missing out on the fun and closeness we experienced as kids. Sadly, there are family members who have no clue they are related, which in turn leads to our children having the same obliviousness. I am one of those people, not knowing everyone I am related to.

My children brought out the drive in me to know more, be great, and open up. It was my mission to make their lives better. This canceled out much of what people thought they knew about me. I advocated my children to being open to getting know everyone, so they can know who they are and where they came from.

Being the first to say I'm sorry is not a sign of weakness, nor is crying. It takes strength to admit defeat and let your guard down. Family is family, regardless of what happens day-to-day, or in the past. I was written off by some family members because all they saw was my addictions and turns I took along the way that they may have heard of and did not look, nor understand the reasons for them. It's imperative to love the ones you love at their best, or at their worst.

I know what it feels like to be looked down upon for not living the way they think you should, and to feel like an outsider. I also know how it feels to be treated you I was a waste of genetics for following my heart (This is a story for later.). It really does something to you inside and you question your importance to the world and to your family. Dealing with life without family and having your children miss out on every opportunity that installed traits in you that made you the person you are is truly hurtful.

There is always time to mend a relationship or mend the family you created. Walking away and throwing in the towel is one of the easiest and simplest ways to solve every problem. It may be time to try something new, something that takes time, and makes you want to give…working at it. Effort put forth moves one even towards mending a relationship. The best things in life always come at a price and are not easy to attain. Family is one of those things worth the fight and family is always worth saving. Yet, it is important to keep your eyes focused on the promise, not the problem.

Chapter Four

Love Changes Things

Finding the one you want to spend your entire life with is not an easy task. Jumping in and out of love can be extremely painful, not to mention a waste of time. In the process this makes damaging soul ties; you never know what spirits someone has attached to them.

Personally, there were many prospects, but none really could handle me mentally, or knew the roads I had taken in my life. I also never took men seriously from childhood's unfortunate events, like I said before. The first instinct for me was to hurt them before they could hurt me, automatically assuming it will come. Plus knowing men are going to be men regardless of how good of a woman you may be. When you have trust issues, relationships are even harder. Trust is a very sensitive issue, easy to obtain but hard to restore. When it is broken, I became a detective, noticing every detail and questioning everything. Checking phones, texting females, or monitoring every move he makes. I exhibited a lack of confidence combined with no trust for anyone. One thing I also learned was to never question the other female but question your partner. If it wasn't for him, they wouldn't be in the picture. Being a detective is not always a bad thing because it uncovers the truth, making it harder for lies to be told to you, if you're thinking clearly that is.

The best part about what seems like making endless mistakes when it comes to love, is when you least expect it, love comes. For me, I actually prayed for him when I was young, literally prayed while passing time with my aunt and uncle on a job they were working; they had the task of cleaning venues after different events at different locations.

This night happened to be his prom night, for the high school I also attended, Destrehan High School. The moment I saw him, I just knew that he was the one for me, immediately falling in love. I told myself and God that he was going to be the father of my kids and my husband one day. After that night, I never saw him again. He ended up changing a lifestyle that could have went on forever when we did finally cross hearts later on. When you're young you believe everyone you meet will be the one to last forever; growing up you realize they all are not meant to be. I was not faithful at all through any of my relationships as a young adult, not many are at that age. That is one of the reasons that led to my faithfulness with the one I asked for that night and the fact I knew it was meant to be just from having what I prayed for by acknowledging that God does answer prayers, no matter how big, or small they may be through my faith.

The strange part of it all is we never were around each other through the years to even feel the way I felt about him, let alone pray for him. I never saw him again until I moved into a place my uncle was renting out in New Sarpy, Louisiana. Being my first official place on my own, having my best friend as my roommate, this was a place I only visited growing up to see my grandmother, or passed through with my father. New Sarpy is where a lot of my family comes from. I never saw him on any of these visits and that's where he is from as well.

So, there I was, clowning around with my family, getting the place in order, and suddenly there he was again with the radio of his mom's car blasting. He looked as though he wanted to get my attention; yet, he didn't know he had caught it a long time ago. Mentally, I was preparing for the close encounter I knew was bound to happen. Something inside me just gravitated towards him, like it was meant for us to be put together at that moment.

After watching him for a while, I made it my mission to get close to him by asking for a ride in his mom's car. Considering, I really did not need one, my mom forewarned him jokingly telling him to watch out, she is trouble. I had to use the fast side of me one last time to obtain the prize, without actually using it completely. (Laughing while I'm writing.) He was the love of my life, calmed me and made me feel safe. From then on, I wanted to be by his side forever.

I found out later that he was he was my mini-stalker in the best way, gave yet another confirmation that you get what you pray for and he wanted me the same way I wanted him.

As we got to know each other through long nights of courting is when I found out he had been watching me through the years. Talk about meant to be, I believe meant to be is an understatement when it comes to him and I. He told me of moments when he saw me, and what I was doing at the moment while living in Destrehan. As sexual as I was back then, I did things differently this time around and waited for it to happen on its own. It actually was perfect, but I still had love for someone else. When he came to town, I put my soulmate to the side wanting my past for all the wrong reasons knowing it really was over before it all happened. My newfound love was not what family wanted for my life; my mother was all for it. He wasn't in college or NBA bound. Luckily, I didn't focus on how much money he had. His heart was big, and he treated me like a lady.

It was Christmas Eve when it became official and it just so happened to snow that year, talk about a love story. I was sitting around with my ex-lover, but my soul was already elsewhere. Unfortunately, I made sure of it, still growing. I think the main reason I really held on so tight to my past lover as long as I did was to not disappoint anyone due to his status in the world, plus that spirit I had inside me wanting to use him. His future was looking very bright and I was there from the beginning. I loved him but he was not the love intended for me; I realized I was no longer in love with him.

My love for him intensified that night and when I completely let go, I had already been watching him the entire day from my living room window. He was riding around with my little brother, which is not weird at all, right? After you try to get rid of any trace of him ever being there. One call that I did make, and I must say being older now I know you treat people the way you want to be treated, was that I had done a lot of praying about it. My soul mate dropped off my past and we had each other from then on.

We were inseparable and many obstacles tested our connection to each other, over and over. From the beginning my father disapproved, and so did many other family members, but with my mother being one of our biggest supporters, I decided to follow my heart anyway. I did not care what the world had to say. Besides the obvious wild nature that I developed had caused a rift in bonds long before that, and it didn't matter what they had to say. What I felt for him and still do feel for him was worth going against the world for. This is my reason why I chose him until the day I die.

Family continued to look down upon us, casting out our love for each other, as puppy love from the beginning. His family supported us as well, understanding our love for each other and our family. Fourteen years put the puppy love theory to shame. I have always been a free spirit and my soulmate ended a life of jumping from one man to the next. All I saw and wanted was him for the rest of my life. Even though there were people who didn't want us together, we made a beautiful family. We made a plethora of magical memories together through our trials. There was one person encouraging me to follow my heart the entire way through, after all I got this heart of mine from a queen. My mother.

Unfortunately, our love was tested again and for the first time in almost two decades we are apart. When you let issues fester without talking about them and lose sight of what's important, one year can change your entire life, then comes the crushing. We have two intelligent and handsome sons, Tavon Walker, Jr. and Trevez Walker. In the end love always prevails and deep in my heart, I feel there is another chapter for us waiting to begin, even if it's to be the closest of friends. We have moved in different directions in life.

One thing I can say about love is you have no control over who is meant to be in your life for the rest of your life. People come as blessings and lessons. Your family has the greatest influence on you, *i.e.* your parents. From the moment you come into this world, they set out to have your best interest and give you the best life they could. Becoming a mother, I also learned some aspects of being a parent you can't control. My children are almost to the age of venturing off finding love and I have the understanding that you can't choose the paths they take; you can only support them regardless of what they decide, while keeping in mind your mistakes to better handle certain situations. Love is never easy and it's not up to family or friends to determine your spouse. Everyone has a past, has a quality some may not see as desirable, basically a reason that makes them unattractive to someone on the outside looking in. Worrying about what other people think will only hurt your relationship. There are people in this world who are not happy with their lives, or themselves, and will say anything to destroy your happiness.

When parents see or feel you haven't reached your potential in life due to the choices you have made in companionship, it can cause many issues. Time is wasted through lack of communication and understanding, that bond is important. Love is never something to be ashamed of and I am a firm believer in love conquering all. I will always love my soulmate and best friend. If I had a chance to change anything I wouldn't. I would do it all over again. Instead of frowning upon choices your loved ones make, understand everyone has a story they overcame. What looks as though they are settling for less than what they deserve is actually a new generation beginning their walk in life. If you feel you have mastered your life and changed it for the better, pull someone to the side and share your wisdom without judgement. Teaching and respecting the journey of others should be a blessing to you. Remembering the past always brightens the future if you keep an open mind and an open heart.

Chapter Five

Blessings in Disguise

When I became a mother my entire life changed, as any mother's life should who truly loves and understands the tasks they are blessed to take on. With that knowledge, each day you become better than the day before through it all. My first child, a son was born November 11, 2006 my oldest, Tavon Walker, Jr. and my youngest is Trevez Walker.

Having two sons is like having mini-adventures on a daily basis, especially with them being so close in age. I have been waiting for the cameras to jump out for a while from the wild and crazy moments we experience, and the mommy moments where your knowledge is being questioned, those moments where like the elders tell you the smarter you get, the dumber I get. (As for me, breaking generational curses is a must and sometimes I Google it if I really can't figure it out after too long with my respect intact. Just how unbelievable some of the moments are. My eldest son and my mother are born on the same day. It is a blessing to have my son born the same day as my mother but also a challenge. When she leaves this world, I will have to be extra strong to celebrate my son's life without mourning my mother's, but with them sharing the same day I can choose to celebrate her life every year without feeling sad; I have the option to be strong. Two sons a year, and three days apart, is a continuous overflow of confirmations.

I had trouble in my body with recurring ovarian cysts, including a scare with the threat of ovarian cancer while I was growing up. I didn't conceive until my early twenties with my soulmate. When I found out I was pregnant, I was ecstatic and their father was certainly even more excited than me at the time. I had been afraid of not becoming pregnant, but I was ready for children, anticipating what I had prayed for.

Children are blessings from God and doing right by them allows your blessings to flow. Even in the most undesirable situations, you have a choice: to have things your own way, or to do what's best for your blessings. Armed with that understanding and feeling as though my family was not fully accepted, I made sure my sons knew who God is and were protected, so they were baptized young. My oldest showed a passion for God and the church also fueled my longing for them to be saved. This was my way of showing them my love on a grand scale and marking a pivotal point in my growth, as not only their mother but their protector, their teacher, their guide, and example. I had made sure they understood the need for God's love, as well as the wisdom that comes along with that love. Their baptism came a couple years after I was baptized on Mother's Day; I did it as an adult but it's never too late for anything.

A gradual change came leading up to my most transforming point in my life. I have brilliant sons who still challenge me every day and the more I search for knowledge and wisdom, I look forward to those days where I ask them to teach me what they know. The world is constantly changing and leaning on your own understanding, or the ones before you, will leave you repeating the same patterns.

Being a mom is not easy. I always say it's one of the hardest jobs a woman can have. Constant worry and questioning if you are even a productive parent are those questions that will always come while seeing accomplishments; they will bring you pride and joy praising them. As a mother, a true mother, you always want more for them. At times there may be the feeling that can hover over you that accuses you, saying you are scarring them as you grow into becoming the proper guardian for them and yourself. You cannot guide you seeds if you do not know where you are going in life. If you are wondering aimlessly, your legacy, your blessings will do the same and so will the ones after them. A manual would have been nice but that's not reality, a helmet too (lol). As a mother, I made mistakes and took a few wrong turns.

When I stepped back and thought about it later on, I actually did well by installing a foundation of love with an appreciation for what you have, even though it may not be what you want. One variable that remained constant was my love for them. I was not able to provide the material things they wanted all the time, but I provided them with knowledge, a voice, respect for others, thrift for different cultures, and affirmations all confirming no dream is unattainable. Loving your children and spending time with them is priceless. The material things do not guarantee they will be emotionally stable, or productive in society, or that you will be.

I have seen many children sitting alone at recreational events, field trips, and wandering the streets getting into trouble, or just wasting time. During my season, my sons were those kids for a short period time, my crushing season, the first time it ever happened. Many of my loved ones felt I sheltered them too much and did not allow them to branch out into the world. I now agree with the partially because knowing what I experienced at a young age, I wanted to protect them.

Additionally, I have kept in mind of breaking those generational curses. Do get me wrong, I am not bashing my family, nor their loved ones. All I know is my story, my truth. When depression fell upon me, I lost sight of my heart and I lost love for self.

My heart also always felt for those kids, as I also understood that working was important in order to provide for your children. I encountered many struggles to provide for my children because I put them first, before any job. So, they know you have support through everything you do. I tested them for gifted classes, and we tried every activity that sometimes came with a feeling of disappointment when it didn't work out. I always still prayed that their passion would come. I also at times switched from one job to the next to fit being a supportive mother and provider in at the same time.

Love is something you can't provide with money. Providing is something that's mandatory when you have children, love is not. Time is precious. There were times when I would let them talk; this made a difference. Also, sitting down at those events just so they see my face (looking at them searching the crowd as confirmation) is a feeling worth any hardship that I had to face. As a consequence, I always encouraged them to have those family game nights until they started to look forward to them. Eventually, they grew to love those activities. Forcing those activities was a head-banging road at times but worth it.

It pains me when I hear someone say a child is corrupt when all they actually need is a little more love and affection. I always tell my sons I love you; they say I'm not cool for a lot of the things I do to stay in tune with them. (I am the cheesy one and proud of it.) I instilled into their minds that they are great. There is no greater agony to me than leaving this world without my sons knowing how much they are loved or watching them live life feeling they have no love. I would rather give them too much love and be the mom they need to tell stop sometimes. They both automatically know what I'm going to say each day when they walk out of the door, nor do I get offended when they just leave.

I loved showing them to follow their dreams; that is the greatest feeling I have ever had in my life. This feeling is so indescribable. We have had a plethora of marvelous memories, but nothing compares to following your dreams and your children are supporting you and watching you. They know they are destined to be king's accomplishing great things. Anything is possible if you set your mind and your heart on it. With simply doing that, you instill everything they need to make them feel that no star is out of reach for them.

The material things will come and being hard on yourself for not providing the material things hurts you and keeps you at a point where you can't focus to even be driven enough to obtain them. Love gives them hope and love keeps them focused even when there is a struggle surrounding them. Keeping yourself together and showing them your strength makes them even stronger. Through my struggles and my journey, my sons have become my foundation, keeping me in line at those moments I feel I am going to fall apart or give up. I am not ashamed to say my sons keep me in line either. What is the point of making them strong if they do not challenge you, or keep you in line? This confirms I am doing right by them.

With that said, there should always be an overflow of love shown to your children because the days that love is not at its highest peak it won't break them or their spirit. Not only will they be okay, they will lift you up as well, instantly knowing you need love on those hard days. They will still carry the positive influence wherever they go. Protect your blessings, give them your time, and treasure every moment spent with them. In a world that is losing compassion for life itself, giving away their blessings, and taking no regard to who they create with the need has never been greater.

Again, it is imperative to break any generational curses and let go of any hindrance that is keeping your love from flowing freely. My sons are two of my greatest blessings and all their lives, they will know from me, their mother that they are not anything less than that, blessings to me.

"For where your treasure is, there will your heart be also." (Matthew 6:21)

Chapter Six

A Mother's Love

A mother's love shelters you through all walks of life. She prays for you day in and day out, allowing you to walk your own path. A mother's love does allow for the making mistakes to mature one into adulthood. That love is a love unmeasurable, a love that has an endless supply to your every need. For those aspects alone, a mother's love should be treasured.

Mothers make the ultimate sacrifice for their children, the chance of losing her life in order to create yours. A mother will take on the world at times to ensure her children's happiness, while compromising her own, even a plethora of times along the way.

They say it takes a community to raise a child and keep them headed in the right direction. Imagine the load one parent has to carry to accomplish this main goal. Keeping their children out of harm's way every day until they are able to fly on their own.

As time goes by, it's easy to begin to take her for granted. The time spent together shortens, the calls are not as frequent, and small gestures to show appreciation are few. I love you does not come as often as it should either. Communication starts to fade from the lack of appreciation, leaving confusion and disagreements. There are also points in time that one may be left wondering what was even the subject of the arguing. Even though they may not say it, it hurts when the close relationship starts to diminish. It plagues them every day, especially if they have lost their own mother. From the moment you are put in your mothers' hands and she looks down upon you, an imprint, a bond like no other is made.

You only have one mother and one chance to show her you care. My heart goes out to the people who have lost their mothers. Once they are gone, you will never have that chance again. There are only memories to remember her by. All the hard times you face without her will make the world seem like a cold and heartless place. As an adult, she can't solve all your problems, or take away the pain you feel.

Understand her love will not always be loving and gentle. They have to keep you focused, keep you from self-destruction. Sometimes it will cut like a knife, crushing you deep inside. That's when you make the change to receive that love again without the long stares and awkward silence, perhaps feeling that something is not being said, or just wanting to say I'm sorry to clear the air. Nothing they do is to hurt you regardless of how it may feel. A mother's love can be constructive criticism in its most loving form.

Cherish her and show her you care. Take time out of the day just to say hi, time is not on anyone's side. The simple things you do matter the most. Spending time cooking and laughing can change your frame of thinking. You can learn things you didn't know and learn how to create better moments from it. It is never too late for change. I put mothers on a platform for one simple reason, (trust me, I understand men can also be single parents), yet can also have it hard.

My mission is to have more appreciation for our women. I believe in giving more concern and care to single mothers, as I know what is going on in the world. Today, the fight is even harder than it has ever been for a single mother. My advice comes as mother myself with a family. I know the drive to guide in the proper direction with so many odds against one is not only challenging, but challenging to our children as well.

Yet, there are some things in life you only get one chance to experience and having a mother is one of those.

Chapter Seven

Struggles

We are all taught growing up that financial stability increases the chances of life actually being fulfilling and rewarding. Without it, prepare for the abundance of tears and many a reason to give up. Being able to provide is the most important aspect of being a mature and productive adult, your purpose right. Who are you if you don't have money? The question is if you don't have the right values and morals along with a right relationship with God that can lead to your own destruction. If you slack on providing (working), it can cause a domino effect of problems. Not only financial, but also mental. The mental is the key to life itself. I have had many jobs throughout my life, a habit of leaving everyone for a better one, or wanting to be there for my sons, touching back on being a mother, I know to many it may seem to be an excuse for laziness, but when you take pride in being a mother in every aspect.

What is truly important and imperative that one consider and is consistent with is the breaking the cycles of generations before you. Not everything is bad, but you have to realize the ones that taught us came from trauma they never truly healed from, so in turn they could not whole heartedly guide us properly without instilling the pain they experienced as well.

Looking back, they needed me to stay at work to bring in what keeps it all together. Trust me, did I work and was a juggler, proudly offered management jobs by everyone I worked for, acknowledging my work ethic; therefore, money is the glue for the vain. If your foundation is built on shaky ground, it will not stand. Although, money does not guarantee happiness.

Another important aspect of adulthood is not depending on others, or the government, therefore turning into a statistic. Racism is not as black and white as it used to be back then but does not make it any less real. Believe it or not, it's up to us to break away from those labels. Not only those of the past but those created, and still generating today. Many people lean on others to keep their children because they are family or friends. In actuality, no one has to help at all. God gave you the responsibility and blessed you with them, knowing you could handle it. Not only children, the gift of life, the reason to wake up every day. In my eyes and my perspective, it's not easy but anything worthwhile or worth having does not come easy.

As you go through it all you are being conditioned, the thing about being conditioned is knowing who you are. If not, the repetitive circle we tend to feel, happening time-to-time, will continue until you recognize it.

I have worked cleaning homes, fast food, waitressing jobs, home health care and security. I have looked for my purpose in the process, all the while inside me, I learned from all the people I have met and gained skills from each one. Labeling myself as an all-around threat (there's a toot there), my first job was at Popeye's at the age of fifteen and I made some valuable relationships, as far as learning and growth, being ready to take on the world at a young age. If you are humble and accept no one is perfect but made perfectly in their own image, you allow yourself to learn. Even the people you feel you may not be able to learn anything valuable from, end up teaching you.

Blessed with many abilities as mentioned before. One of the numerous gifts I was blessed with was the ability to do hair. We all have different abilities and I am not being racist but as an African American woman, we pride ourselves on learning. Being able to accomplish many different feats. I developed that passion watching my mother, and my aunts. Those talents were not limited to just the beautiful adult women in the Thomas family, it trickled down to us all having the same ability, beauty - a passion for us all. As a child one of my favorite Aunt's house was one of my favorite places to be because she had her own salon in her garage that she built herself. I washed hair when she needed me too, or grabbed a product that she needed to complete a client she was working on. In the process, doing nails with my older cousin, or trying new things, I learned many gifts, but still never realized my purpose in life, or accepted it.

During those work hiatuses, I encountered countless struggles, for good reason. You can't know there is a ninety percent of rain with a chance of tornados and not expect it to storm. Having to move when the money ran low repeatedly, feeling less of a woman each time it happened. Living paycheck-to-paycheck, scraping up change from the purse just to buy snacks, having a partner is not what you lean on; it is important to make each other better. Every woman needs to be the driving force of her family not afraid to admit falling short can make you to feel inadequate. I can never say I didn't give it my all every time the chips fell because I am a fighter. I never give up with anything I do while keeping a sickening positive attitude. People wonder how she smiles so big and we heard this, or family knows the

46

struggle. For example, keeping my faith for irresponsibility, knowing everything happens for a reason, even when we don't know the reason at the time. There still is one, always. Knowing you are trying put a clear perspective on it all and I'm an optimist with a duffle bag full of faith, always have been.

I am constantly telling myself everything happens for a reason, which is an uplifting aspiration, therefore sometimes contemplating on mistakes and searching for the reason. Learning from it, I know my family would receive something better in time.

Self-doubt is the core of all failures, not believing you are capable of being great, equals fear. Through it all, I have learned loss makes you better and keeps you reaching higher each time you fall, creating a humble heart along the way. Appreciating what you have from only having those resources to work with. You can't receive greater if you'd not know and appreciate the value of what you have.

Being a strong woman made me able to sustain the toughest of times. Praying, keeping God close to me even though I don't regularly attend church. I have developed my own relationship with Him, as everyone should. Never have been short on faith, which is the driving force besides my family. I never claim to be perfect or want to be. You won't find me falling out in the front of the church. I don't want to sound judgmental because I am not simply stating how I feel. My views, the First Amendment, we all have the right to exercise. It also makes me uncomfortable (question the purpose of it), when I see hands being laid on others. I protect my energy and know God made me perfect in His own image, so there is no need for no other hand to be laid on me but His. You are the Church before there ever was a church; you are your own temple. Faith keeps you going when it all seems to fall apart at the seams.

One thing is for certain, everyone goes through the same issues just different variables to them and one struggle is not greater than another. Looking around you feeling as if the world is passing you by from seeing the blessings of others. What glitters is not always gold? The first mistake we make during our season is measuring your journey or walk with what's meant for someone else. Everything that happens in your life is meant for you. Idolizing someone else is misdirection; they are holding pain inside as well, dealing with their own demons. It doesn't matter who you are; we have all faced our own demons and had to overcome them. If there are not any blessings flowing the fact is, you're not doing something right. There is something that needs to change. I know from experience the change is oneself. One answer is breaking away from uncertainty, lack of confidence and a broken down spirit that causes one to have to fight tremendous battles. The battles will remain the same until one looks inside themselves and decides to make a change.

Counting on the people around you is only a minor fix to a problem on a larger scale; when I say minor, this is not a solution at all. An old saying of "throwing sugar on it" so to speak comes to mind. Owning your part in the circumstances in your life that you create is the only way to come out victorious, thereby placing blame on the only one who is in control of every outcome, you.

There is always a breaking point when you question every decision you have ever made in life, remembering all the wrong turns you've made. I have had that pivotal moment happen in my own life and it opened better doors. Do not despair, during that time is the best moment to search for your purpose and build on your relationship with

God. This will give you the drive and courage that you need to turn it all around. By allowing the pain to lift you up when it's hard because in the end when you put in the work the outcome will be worth every stone you had to face; therefore, one can turn immense pain into power.

Confidence will come knowing you did it on your own from determination, endurance, and the will to be great. That determination will forever remain when you begin to see the progress you are making from it. This is a lifestyle of change. It's imperative to keep going when you don't see progress in the beginning. Once you see the difference around you from change, you will not want to stop.

Losing is not an option anymore, only conquering and keeping in mind how far you've come, while never forgetting where you came from. Elders use the term, instilling it in us, hitting rock bottom. This is when your money is gone, and you have nowhere to turn to. I can say that I hit rock bottom, but it wasn't due to money being gone, my faith was gone. I don't believe in hitting rock bottom, that's how I know my faith was depleted. I believe every day is a new opportunity. Opening your eyes is the first blessing we have each day and that alone shows us how blessed we are, fueling each day with a positive mindset.

Maintaining and focusing on what's to come is the attitude one must take, instead of the losses we have experienced. They are experiences and lessons that we have learned from. Each day is a new day, and another chance to be better than you were yesterday. The lifestyle or life you desire will not come to you on a platter; you have to pick yourself up and go get it. Faith and prayer also light the way for an exciting journey.

Chapter Eight

Shape Shifter

Through my life I have been taught a hard lesson in how everyone does not have the same heart. Not everyone looks at love and life through simplistic lenses. Their loyalty is determined by materialistic value and measured by the pain they experienced in the past. We are told constantly to stop crying when life attempts to knock us down, crying is seen as a sign of weakness. When you cry coming from struggle you have to suck it up and keep going because if you cry too long it consumes you. Hindering you, blurring your vision only able to focus on the source of the pain on a daily basis, making one handicapped in a sense.

Crying is a release to me, not a weakness. Crying releases the pain and keeps stress from taking you over, especially if there is no one you feel you can relate to. Always keep in mind you are never alone. Crying and acknowledging the reason for the pain while being completely honest with yourself in the process, alone and having an admittance session is the best way for me to process my heart. It has to get worse before it can get better. The hard truth produces the best outcomes, true growth. Not lying to yourself putting or putting a band-aid on the wound, soothing the pain for a later day.

Unfortunately, a day will come that is a pileup of the recurring circumstances that life throws your way. It can tear you down mentally and physically and keeping those emotions all bottled inside turned me into someone I couldn't recognize when my crushing came. My uncle once said the first thing people remember when they think back on their lives are the traumatizing events. I also wanted to say people remember how an event made them feel, or how someone made them feel from the way they are treated.

This can bring on unjustified criticism from not saying what is going on inside one's thoughts and feelings. At some point, that criticism I was hearing from the ones I loved began to play back in my mind daily. As it played with no outlet, I started to shape shift, being who I needed to be around certain people, feeling as thought I did not have a voice. The woman whom I wanted to be was screaming for someone to listen. So, instead of forcing people to listen, I decided to be the change I wanted to see and let my change speak for itself.

The shift was not intentional but came from not wanting to disappoint them. Becoming afraid to be myself, with having compassion and respect for the ones you love, or that are placed in your life, disappointment is not an option. With a certain level of trauma, you do have mental scars and pleasing others is a direct effect of it; it is a defense mechanism. I lost sight of who I was at the time; I let all the pain go and forgot about it for many years. This was thanks to a love I never felt before, protection.

Now I am free to be a part of myself, and I say "part" because true freedom doesn't come until I let it all go. I have learned being yourself attracts the people who really value who you are as a person. If you have to work too hard at it, or are always feeling you have to prove yourself, it is not the right environment for you, or are they the ones you need in your life. I now have the pleasure of reintroducing myself and through my book, *Words Unspoken,* as I present to you the new and improved me, without a question, I am still me.

During this part of my storm, I became an introvert, sheltering myself from the outside world. I felt as though my world was caving in, for a year I did but I did not. I was simply existing, not living, wondering and watching. Relationships went into an almost oblivious state, blocking what could have been many blessings (maybe) or maybe not. Everyone that says they are looking out for you, that truly has your best intentions, sit back and compare and contrast without having a spirit of jealousy, or any of the other factors that reflect insecurity. Compare and contrast in an intellectual light helps you come to a sensible conclusion to problems. Not comparing your walk to others but simply having the understanding is a must because you don't envy, are jealous, or have cruel intentions to destroy others. That does not apply to everyone.

I was stuck in my own way of holding onto past negativity and becoming a bipartisan hypocrite in regard to my own beliefs of family being the most important thing. You have to accept, as well, even though you don't speak on everything you go through, that does not mean people do not see. The thought from where I come from, *that I'm going to mind my business complex is one of the main reasons people tend to hold a lot in,* as the saying goes. I am one of the few people who will sit down with you and ask if you want to talk. As many can see I can keep secrets, so everyone who has come to me with their secrets are just that. Loyalty is royalty, and again, I held a lot in, and I didn't share, so I know how it feels to not want a conversation exposed to anyone else. I would have only done that if I trusted someone enough to express my feelings to. We all need at least one person we can confide in outside of God. He (God) does make it better and He is the most trustworthy,

52

but if we start building better foundations for relationships, not assuming the worst out of everyone, relationships will be built. Discernment allows you to know who and when, you do need a who and when from time to time.

Going into the world again, I was afraid my shame was visible to them, unleashing all the trauma that was buried underneath the surface. Losing what I held most precious to me triggered it as well. Realizing all the mistakes I had made, amounted to much shame. I thought of everything that had been done to me, all equaling, shame. I realized I had wasted time by not using the gifts I was blessed with by God to better myself, or family, again, more shame shed its dark shadow upon me. This shame heightened so high above me that when I began to search for God and my purpose, it was difficult and confusing.

To elaborate on this, let me speak about judgement in my family, knowing my past and growing from what I went through. At the same token, I had wondered what would be said about my "spiritual awakening." Sometimes you have been spoke of so much and judged by family that it comes to a certain point that seems to be impossible to undo the judgment that has been cast upon you, no matter how much you have changed. They do not want to be wrong.

They have to save face and need a grand gesture of sorts to really prove you are who you say you are now. The one's who judge the most tend to have the most skeletons. They know they are trustworthy, so it is hard to believe anyone else.

I had lost confidence in myself, not knowing what to do around them, even a simple smile or hello felt awkward from those words unspoken. Everyone is not able to expose the things they feel that might bring on undesirable attention and judgement. Holding on can cause you to question your reality, no longer being able to differentiate what is real from lying to yourself, or from the pain you haven't dealt with.

The worst feeling is going into society again, not knowing which way to turn, feeling as though you want to run away. Facing the fact, you need to be there for them and yourself. Not allowing them to see you as broken, loving the life you live, and gripping the changes you're facing even when it's hard. God gives His strongest battles to His strongest soldiers. Jumping back into it with the fear in your heart makes you even the stronger and equips you with more than enough to face the adversities you created.

You never know who can shed light in the darkest corners of your mind. I battled with having to cast down negative thoughts from holding onto the past for a long time. All the while, still living and enjoying life, and living purposely. I have a joy for living and it's hard to believe I went to a place I did not want to be around anyone.

On my journey to greatness, I learned a valuable lesson, allowing people to be there for you will open doors that will give you hope and bring you out of those dark places if you allow them in. Pray for a spirit that knows the difference and for God to surround you with the people you need. I gave it to God and to a couple that I felt God led me to, by whom I have been inspired by while they were uplifting me in the process. A bishop and First Lady from New Sarpy, Louisiana, known the Kenner's, a true power couple in my eyes.

In regard to progress and self-destruction; it's not only hard for you but hard for the ones who love you to sit back and watch the self-destruction. There is no such thing as mind readers and a closed mouth does not get fed. I know everyone has possibly heard that. There are worse things that can happen, like not having anyone at all and slowly watching life take loved ones away from you without having those talks or sharing those moments that keep you from the brink of insanity.

What is important to do is to start replacing the negative feelings and thoughts, allowing the positive to take control. Giving you the boost you need to say, "I'm going to brush it off and keep moving." When life makes you want to run away, that's the time to stand tall and fight for the life you are meant to live! The enemy does not attack just anyone; it attacks greatness. Thank God for it.

Chapter Nine

Rebirth

I have explored and have been continuously working on perfecting the lifestyle skills that I have learned to correct the issues I was dealing with "mentally and physically." Now, if those outlets, which turned into a new way of living could change me, giving me a whole new outlook on life, it can also help someone else. Meditation on the Word is one of the habits I have formed and practice daily. Meditation on the good things of the Lord, and His promises are a way to improve mind, body and health. Yes, this will promote "positive" thinking and allow one to receive washing from the Word, that will create positive attitudes to flow. In a practical way, one has to work out in their own mind what they allow into their minds, as well as what they think.

In respect to physical health, improving my body, committing to working out three days a week, loving who I see when I look the mirror. We are created in His image and it's important to love yourself. Only you know what you need to be the best version of yourself. With all the unhealthy choices shoved in our faces from social media, commercials, and fast food restaurants everywhere; there are many choices. We have to go the extra mile to protect our temples. Both became addictions for me due to all the insecurities that built up through time.

Over confidence (pride) can truly keep you from striving to achieve a better life. If you feel you do not need an improvement, you will remain stuck in the state, you are. While seeing the vast ways to improve yourself, pride and envy can cause you to look at them and say, "I don't need it and they are not any different from me." One way others might be different is the true love for self, not just blindly loving self. We have to inspire ourselves to get up and get out. Eventually a lifestyle change forms and you will be just as proud of yourself as I am of myself.

My journey to self-improvement started off as wanting to prove people wrong, and also hating what I saw when looked into the mirror. Actually, I had days where I passed them up in disgust, me of all people, anyone that knows me can catch that and get a little laugh out of it. Turning pain into power is one of my strengths, as should be us all. Work through it and laugh at it later.

We all have looked in the mirror at some point in time, longing for the youthful version of ourselves as age sets in. A constant positive in life, and a refreshing one, is we can change it all at any given time. At my worst, I weighed two hundred and fifteen pounds.

Imperfections were all I saw when I looked in the mirror; with the same token knowing I have beauty within. Before I started truly taking care of myself, I encountered different infections, respiratory illnesses from smoking, abscesses, which formed for many different reasons, skin discoloration, and thinning hair. The solution that we have been programmed to seek out is medical attention, not a productive solution to all health issues. In no way am I saying do not seek medical attention when you need it; I just wanted to suggest there might be solutions, other than medical that will helps solve the medical problems one does have.

When I was at my worst, my self-esteem became almost non-existent, not caring what I wore, what I put into my body, and not keeping my hair up as well. Picking myself back up, I shed thirty-four pounds that made a world of a difference. It made me stronger and it builds your confidence.

It takes a lot of effort and determination. It is important to wake up every day and push yourself, even when you feel the pain flowing through every part of your body. Having the strength to keep going, therefore focusing on the outcome being greater than the task at hand. Remembering where you came from, going out in public, and having people unable to recognize you from the tremendous changes made. It does get easier as time goes by. For me, even when I'm stressed, I want to go sweat it out besides the days that are set aside for working out.

Getting fit has health and mental benefits. What a wonderful journey it is to participate in reinventing oneself and to not focus on how others would perceive it due to the past. When I had started losing weight, I knew that the first thing people would think of me was that I was abusing drugs, giving that as the reason I lost so much weight. Unfortunately, others gave no regard to the time, effort, or work that I put into losing the weight. In life, we will always face undue criticism, regardless of doing the right thing. Some people are just programmed that way and haven't dealt with their own issues in life, so it's easier to focus on others to keep from dealing with who they see when they look in the mirror. Dramatic change brings on tremendous opinion; I smile and feel secure in the fact that you never have to explain yourself to anyone; the truth always reveals itself.

It actually pushed me harder just knowing there are skeptics who believe you can't do it, taking the anger you feel in moments like those, and in a productive fashion, can change your life. The anger sneaks in when your hard work is being questioned, although staying humble is a strenuous task at times. After the weight loss, I was at a point where I started to feel comfortable again with who I was. However, I developed a big head, and in swooped vanity. It had been over a decade since I looked and felt that good and going through my storm, I longed for attention. I did not realize it until someone I loved began to find me unattractive, leaving me in complete disbelief. How can this person find me unattractive when I am looking the best I have in years?

The answer is simple, attitude. I was no longer humble, as I cared so much about how I looked. I lost my humbleness for a split-second in time. It really gave me a reality check.

Part of my preparation, another lesson I needed to learn. Flashing yourself is never attractive because you never know what the next person is dealing with. When I say flashing, I mean bragging, moving in silence and choosing what to say and not to say, is the purest form of humbleness.

The struggles I faced myself before the vanity came, made me forget where I was came from. Don't get me wrong, I do know I am great, but I am truly humbled now, more than ever. I always have been humble, but after reaching a point where I had complete confidence again, then thinking back on how I felt at my worse for a season, that can destroy you or your relationships with others. God created us to flourish in life, and not just to survive.

Now God has changed me into a person who loves to help people, gives her last, and lives as though there is a song to each day. I still do have my bad days but somedays, not every day, turned into a vanity monster. Humbleness is imperative; it can turn a beautiful person with the purest of heart into a complete monster. Reflecting someone other than the real you. Please believe some images are harder to break once you have made your mark on people.

I started researching on meditation through the suggestion of one of my closet cousins. I had no clue what I was doing in the beginning, trying almost anything, on a search for mental peace. All I knew was I wanted all the negative energy I had harnessed throughout the years and the pain from the past to go away. What I desired the most was a life that was to be preparing me for a life of promise according to the Word of God.

The Lord led me to becoming a published author, and stepping into a whole new life, a better one, but still entirely new territory to me. Writing this book was a tremendous and tedious task for me that was incredibly rewarding and wonderful therapy as well. I was bringing everything back up to the surface, all the emotions, trauma that I had stuffed deep down inside me and dealing with it all productively, so I could accomplish the goal of writing my book that I set out to achieve, which was God's Will as well. In this way, I did not turn to the outlets, as I once did before.

Once I began everything, all that I had been through in my life weighed me down for a while, but I prayed my way through. I had constant conversations with God, in which God brought healing through getting it out alone with Him.

Confession and repentance played a huge role in admitting each life event and the affect it had upon my heart and mind. There was no sugar coating, or labeling it, I spent time crying through the pain, and worked on my story so that my testimony could benefit others.

The meditation process with God was tedious, and I wanted to quit many times feeling like I was talking to myself, waiting for the Lord of the Universe to respond back to me. I told myself, *okay Tronell, you're going to end up in the nut house*, but immediately shook that off with the confirmation that if anyone tried to take me, I would be driving back while they were being processed. I considered myself much too smart to be insane or mentally ill. So, I started inside. Positive thinking made it easier, reminding myself of a positive image, or positive word, and then I focused on it. As I recall, everything I went through in the process of my rebirth and my search for God was the source of my comfort as well. Those long talks with Him paid off. For a while I felt God was the only one I could lean on and talk to, seeing the progress that is the way He needed it to be.

I can't stress enough that you do not have to feel guilty about the relationship you have with God or feeling you don't have one because people do not see you in church every Sunday; that is shame. The most important part is having a relationship with God. You don't have to be perfect, or speak in tongues, nor be ashamed of what you've been through. Embrace your walk, your story. You are never too far out of reach. Reaching a certain level in your faith you understand the importance of being in attendance and acknowledging God for the blessings in your life; it should not be forced. Everything happens according to God's plan. Everyone does need a home, wait for it.

Soon enough I had formed another lifestyle change, piling on self-help books. These days, I focus on reading more and more, remembering simple things in life that bring me the most joy, meanwhile not allowing the changes, or negativity around me to change who I am. The woman I lost through not being able to let go of the past, or talk about how I felt inside, is worth the woman I became. I was lost, but now I am proud of knowing how it feels compared to before; I want this feeling that I have now forever and would not choose to go back to how I was when I was lost. I have had many blessed moments and memories along the way, enough to keep me pressing forward.

Going through a separation of the entire process of letting go of my marriage and the idea of a perfect life, which took months to climb out of the sadness it brought me. The loss I was experiencing in my life at this time was also another reason for shutting out the world. I went to the doctor and was prescribed a small coffee table of medicine, that I ended up throwing away before the third day. I viewed that situation as God has a reason for everything and I didn't need them. I kept meditating on Him and focused on what can go right instead of what was going wrong or could go wrong.

Though losing family, or the people you love is hard, I was empowered. This was a chance to make it happen on my own and show the world I am a strong woman with tremendous faith. I purchased my first car and moved my sons and I to a home on our own. God had to isolate me to build me up again. This was the way He intended me to be.

I started out five days week walking what felt like miles leaving the stress and pain on the pavement; now it's for a healthy lifestyle. When the battle is won, the fight is not over, but going through it all, finding comfort, I also found my joy for food again. It was a mindset change, wanting a better life, and committing to the lifestyle change. Drinking lemon water to flush anything not meant to be inside my body was also part of my health regime. The taste takes time to get used to, but the benefits are far greater the negative aspect of drinking something sour. I recommend the fruit to everyone; it helps with weight loss and without the waist trainers or starving yourself (dieting). I had begun to love myself wholeheartedly, and was confident in the growth to come, correcting what I felt needed to be corrected.

I began trusting God more and more each day, leaving the need to meditate at almost a standstill, only when I felt my mind and heart needed to be realigned. In other words, when I felt that life became too much to handle for any given reason, the relaxation it brings you when you feel overwhelmed is priceless.

If life knocks you down a thousand times, you have to get up a thousand and one. The enemy (Satan) wants to steal your joy. Not everything in your life is meant to keep you from getting to your destination, step back and refocus. There is no such thing as failures, only tests of your faith to see if you will give up on what matters the most. What should matter most to you should be God's plans for your life, which comes with many blessings and God-birthed dreams.

"Watch ye, stand fast in the faith, be brave, quit you like men, be strong." (1 Corinthians 16:13 KJV)

Chapter Ten

Purpose

Music throughout history has been referenced to as the language of love. Music can take you to different places, as you relate to your emotions to each word of the song. People listen to music, but I feel it with every chord, drum beat, bass tone, or those distant chimes only an artist ears can catch when it hits the soul. As one works past the aches and pains through the music, not only sad emotions release, but music also offers a boost on the days when you need a boost. With that said, speak to when life is not going the way you planned. For lack of a better phrase, when everything and everyone is getting on your last nerve, music can happen to even bring calm.

Mariah Carey and Mary J. Blige was, and still are, two of my favorite artists for inspiration. The emotion they put into their music and the way they carry it out takes me away. They also have a story behind the music. Following not only the music of artist but their life also. There is a story behind the music, which makes all artists great. Some of the best artists come from the most pain. They are seductive, strong and smart.

I like listening to anything from Gospel music to R&B, to Rock and Roll, like the Rolling Stones, The Beatles, In Sync, and Sade, the list can go on and on. To be a true lover of music and art you have to love it all without restrictions. In my own space, in my room, with my thoughts, pen, and paper, when you feel no one listens to you, it creates a bigger voice inside you.

Knowing that now, I enjoy being alone and would rather put a pen to my thoughts than speak them at all. I still am very vocal though. I am way too straight-forward sometimes seeming borderline to cold. It was not until I matured as an adult, that I accepted the fact that I always had someone listening to me. I just was not talking about the issues I needed to talk about or did not trust anyone with my thoughts. During that time, I lost my passion for music, writing and art. I am thankful there is always a light at the end of the tunnel and my inspiration returned.

Sometimes you know there is a calling on your life, but you refuse to get out of the way. It took for me to have to go through a complete 360 in my life, and to feel I was at my lowest point, to find my love for art again and my voice. Discovering my faith in God again as well, that feeling on and off that He is not who people say He is was gone and is gone. When you go through enough, it's easy to forget all God really does for you. Asking if God saw so much in me, I had to ask "why" did any of the trials I faced have to happen, owning that He gives His toughest battles to His strongest soldiers.

I recall one of my toughest battles happened as I sat in my mother's backyard the day of my birthday, January 7, 2018. I was trying to keep my spirits up while receiving a flood of negativity from places you wouldn't expect it from on a day meant to celebrate your life. I was thankful for my mother who made it better with a ride to the store, grabbing a few of my favorites, and for the people who still reached out with well wishes. On top of this I had an internal battle going on, stepping into completely unfamiliar territory. I was remembering who I was, embracing who I was becoming, and letting go of many pieces who I once was.

I could not even handle my sons at the moment, so I removed myself for a while to regroup. I grabbed a chair, my phone charger and a drink, still a work in progress at the time, on a mission to handle the day. Turning music on to comfort me, at that time Gospel was all I wanted. Couldn't listen to anything else, I tried to. I attempted to sing a couple of songs before I had a breakthrough with this one song, I played repeatedly called, "Break Every Chain" by Tasha Cobbs. The thought of God relieving the pain and breaking the chains that weighed me down fueled my conviction.

Listening to this song, had sparked a deep longing inside me, if I sang loud enough and felt it strong enough, I would be free. As the song began to play, I had a heart full of sadness I wanted to wash away. I looked to the sky and poured my heart out. I did not have a care in the world about the fact I could be disturbing the peace. I had closed off my voice to household cleaning, and the fun and games. Before it all happened, I prayed I not to lose my gift, my voice. I sung so loud as if I wanted God to hear me. Never was I able to "let go" on a scale that large, feeling every word and loving what I heard. I felt every word; if I haven't learned anything else, I have learned that even when you think you're not talking to God, you truly are. We can talk to God through prayer, praise, music and the words you speak.

I continued singing, even looked around as I sang through the breaks checking to see of anyone was around proceeding on with the small concert, I was holding in the backyard by myself. Once the song ended, my entire day changed and my outlook on life as well. I was still dealing with unfavorable circumstances, but not full of worry or sorrow.

In December of 2017, I set out to use my voice by writing my first book. This was a dream I had since I was young. Envisioning myself as many great titles through my writing. The thought of being in the same category as the great women before me such as Mayo Angelou, Shakespeare and a legacy of others gave me a longing that I had but never followed through on. It took a lot of soul searching and realizing who I was again. I had writings from my childhood setting with no home and a story to tell, with another unfolding daily.

It takes long nights of five to six hours of thinking and getting your thoughts out on paper. Then there were days of turning around and going to work after no sleep. There were days of reading endlessly, finishing one and grabbing another. There were also confirmations along the way to not give up this time no matter how hard it became. Singing that day gave me confirmation I was on the right track; this is exactly what you are meant to do and be. I almost put down my pen again before that day, thankfully this time it did not happen.

Acknowledging God's presence, I see why that day was important in my journey. That one day in that chair gave me more patience than before. Music, my relationship with God, my family, health and writing became my sources of inspiration once again. Thirty-four and longing for a creative and successful life, the pause I put on my life and career is finally over. I have come to expect a life with filled with purpose and promise.

The journey is not an easy task; I have had many sleepless nights doubting myself. Feeling inadequate at times and shaking it off. Falling in love with reading again, books are a part of the art. You can open a book and find many things, go to many places, or get swept away fueling inspiration. I love to write, but my dedication for reading took a little more work to obtain again from all the modern technology access, promoting laziness.

The key to committing to reading was reading about subjects I am passionate about. Researching what it takes to be an author and reading the books in the same genre as mine. Wondering what makes me able to write a book giving my life to the world, pretty much was the entire beginning of the process. How can someone who is not perfect teach anyone anything about life, with so many wrong turns, and with so many sins? The answer is simple; I am not teaching but sharing my experiences and how I overcame them as a source of inspiration for someone who went through or may be going through similar events.

From my standpoint and what was put in my heart, someone needs to know that it is never too late. One has to have the courage to be great and one has to fight through it all. I never dreamed that I would give myself a way to inspire others, but I feel a great sense of reward from it. This brings me to tears every time I think about it. I was thinking somewhere on the lines of realistic fiction but what better way to truly inspire than to show people you have overcame every obstacle set before you. I'm just like you and I am not afraid to tell the world about it to help you follow your dreams.

Stand up and give God a chance to show you the way you are meant to go. It just might amaze you and open a whole new world that makes your face hurt from smiling so much.

My frame of mind has changed and the addictions I clung onto that kept me chained, I no longer desire. They do not hold me hostage anymore. It doesn't matter what the addiction is, they all are labeled the same. Honesty is the best policy. It takes courage and wisdom to acknowledge life for what it is and start living the way it should be. One moment can change the direction of your life preparing you for the next level. What will you do with the last bit of adrenaline you have left when it's time for a change in your life on a grand scale and that's usually the time that matters the most? The moment that can turn it all around, *fight or flight*, I hope you choose to fight.

Chapter Eleven

Enjoying the Walk

My walk has taken me to different places, and I am making sure it does. Letting go of the fear of the unknown, my relationships are becoming stronger in the process of preparing for the life I want to live. There are bumps along the way but who wants a perfect life.

Without those hard times you will not learn, the hard days cause you to think and look back on what you do not want to happen again. I am now living a life with no regrets and going to places I have never been and taking chances to create the moments that last a lifetime. When I say "chances" I mean letting go of what people are going to think or say, just living for yourself and not the people around you or what they expect of you.

I am spending more time with my family and friends, making new ones along the way as well. Taking the daily walk of transforming my life for the better of my children's lives, loving someone else regardless of who it is without loving yourself fully will not bring the results you desire out of the relationship.

Going on the field trips I stopped attending, the first one was to an insectarium with my oldest son and his father. I really looked forward to it being a lover of butterflies. I was able to walk around watching them flutter around, mesmerized by the Asian feel that the garden had. Waiting for one to land on me without any luck, wasn't until I gave up the thought that one landed next to my boot. Simple things in life can bring you the most satisfaction.

The highlight of the trip for me was when I was ready to try new things, so I went a step further eating two different types of insects. Anyone that knows me knows how much I despise certain insects, short for afraid of the vast majority. Mealworm salsa and a cricket, another notch under my belt leading me to a carefree life, while also earning the cool and creepy mom badge at the same time.

The adventures do not stop there, I really busted out of my shell with another field trip with my youngest to the wetlands. My son and I walked through a tent set up with pythons down the entire table being held by high school and middle school kids. My curiosity led me to ask how they could handle them, defanged and trained. That was a "lightbulb moment", moving on... As I made my way pass them my curiosity peaked once again (see the pattern) and an albino python caught my eye and before I knew it, he was wrapped around my hand. Absolutely terrified of snakes, I felt fearless, which is the feeling I aim for nowadays. Opening up to new heights, knowing that I had made memorable moments, while strengthening the bond with my sons was priceless moments that are carved in your heart.

A friend of mine who also has a love for artistry hosted an event, "Positive Vibes Poetry." I was amazed by the different ways they expressed themselves through music, poetry, and song fueled inspiration. I felt as if I was broadening my mind to the many different forms of expression. Focusing on what each person was actually saying and analyzing for deeper meanings, was well put together and full of artistry. Those moments were very spiritual as well. It seems as though everything is better with God in it. This is just an example of one of many to come in the future.

I am excited about the new places my life change will bring me. It's imperative to surround yourself with your passion. Having motivation all around you to keep you focused and give you something to strive for. Even reminders of why you started pursuing whatever you decided to do in the first place. There are a melting pot of reasons to set out to be better but having motivation is one reason that sets your soul on fire, giving you determination.

Enjoying the walk the entire way, loving the progress being made in my life. The journey has been flooded with confirmations. Networking was going to be a whole new world for me and since everyone was going to read my life story, why not have a running start. Winning second place in a poetry contest did just that. The fear I feel when I know I am about to do something that normally I wouldn't dream of, I push even harder to accomplish it. The first time in my adult life entering a contest with my work, on the internet for the world to see. Putting my heart out there and seeing what comes back to me. Preparing for the critics that will come in the future in the process.

What I received was unbelievable, not only did I win second place, I inspired people. There were comments left calling me amazing, brilliant, noting that my words were touching to them and that others were able to relate to them, gave me a feeling like no other feeling in this world. This was one of my main purposes for sharing my life and my walk. If even I can inspire only one person, I feel as though my purpose has been fulfilled.

My relationships with my siblings are improving due to better communication. The best remedy for building is not forcing it, allowing the fun moments to happen and appreciate them as they come. As crazy as it may seem to some people, I thank God for the bad times, the bad relationships, and what I don't have. It all comes together eventually. Having moments with your family singing karaoke together in the garage, taking walks with your mother to stay healthy, or relaxing outside swinging together. Those moments replace the distance and confusion.

I have beautiful nieces and nephews, who I try to spoil on holidays anyway I can. With so many of them, it's not an easy task and with some of them not around, some can be left out. I am looking forward to being able to provide more for them all. My relationships with my parents have also become even better, giving them a daughter, they can be proud of. Respecting each other as adults and understanding the decisions you make can affect others, also provides a steppingstone. Every day we all should be building. I am committed to bettering all aspects of my life and there is emphasis on my relationships because everyone needs someone. We are not meant to walk through life alone. Once you build your relationship with God, then move outward to your home, then family and to your friends. My walk has just begun and the changes and blessings I have seen already have blown my mind. Imagining what's to come keeps me on the edge of my seat. All you need is a vision.

The Conclusion

Perfectly Flawed

I am sharing my journey with you to show anyone who has lost their way and gave up hope to keep trying! Change your mind and change your life. The dark places I have been in my life I never shared with anyone but God. He is the only One Who knows everything.

I went through it though and thankfully my mother was always my go to ear for many issues. There still are too many things I held back from the ones I love. In no way am I perfect, along my way, I have had setbacks and lessons I continuously have to learn.

My faith and searching for answers caused God to lift me up and bless my heart, as well as my efforts. Along the way a constant prayer is for Him to guide my steps and for His will for my life to be done. You do not have to be the loudest in the church, or present at every single service, for God to love you or move in your life. Every scripture I read and everything I know about God is love. He knows your heart.

Your past does not define your future, or where you are destined to be in life. The past is called "the past" is also to be left there and learned from. The past sometimes can be a guiding tool for you to live the life you are meant to have.

I am living proof that God can reach you from anywhere you are and pull you out of anything. All you need is to take the first step and allow change to come in and take hold of your life. Change is scary, but how can you grow repeating the same patterns? I am now the woman God intended me to be and blossoming more every day. If it's your season to be taken to the next level, you will be rewarded along the way. Not with money or wealth that comes from material things, for no amount of money can compare to the satisfaction that God gives. Meanwhile, keeping a kind heart that wants to reach out to help others, passing on what you have learned is important. If we have enough people thinking that way, it can cause a change in the world, one heart at a time. When you are being blessed, I believe it is a duty to be a blessing to others.

I am now no longer afraid of judgment, setbacks, making mistakes or falling short. Everyone falls short and when God has more to work with, the story ends with a testimony. Those stories are the best ones regardless of what occurs in life. Everyone loves a happy ending. Sometimes you have to create it after being given a life that's gives you a testimony.

You can't shine without a little darkness.

Look Deeper

Life is what you make it

God gave it to you therefore no one can take it

Even though no one seems to understand it

It's given to you and only you can handle it

The stars are aligned

Keep faith everything happens for a reason

He gives the hardest battles to his strongest soldiers Stay true

This is your season

The stones you create on your own and some not your own

Are stepping stones

Never give up rise above it all reclaim your throne

This life is yours and yours alone

No one can tell you how or when

It is your own

Be fearless be brave even if you have to break a few hearts along the way

The story starts off simple but creates a wave

Embrace who you are and the story will change

Faith and the Universe can give you the muscle to survive

To you I say when the clouds of darkness show their face

Look to the heavens faith without work is dead

Tomorrow is always a brighter day

(September 2018 2nd place contest winner)

Tronell Walker

Made in the USA
Columbia, SC
02 March 2022

56746721R00043